THE OFFICIAL
LIVERPOOL FC
ANNUAL 2013

Written by Paul Eaton

Designed by Brian Thomson

A Grange Publication

ISBN 978-1-908925-08-4

£7.99

Contents

06............................ Season Review

14.... Brendan Rodgers – New Manager

16.....Carling Cup Final Picture Special

18.............................Steven Gerrard

20 .... Liverpool FC Legends on New Boss

22.......................... Jordan Henderson

24................... New Signing: Joe Allen

26...........................José Enrique

28............... 120 Memorable Moments

36............................. Martin Skrtel

38....................................... Crossword

39................................. Wordsearch

40............................... Martin Kelly

42........................... Raheem Sterling

44.................. New Signing: Nuri Sahin

48............... New Signing: Fabio Borini

50..................................... Lucas Leiva

52..... Luis Suarez – Goal-den Moments

54.............................Jonjo Shelvey

56................................ Glen Johnson

58...................... Spot the Differences

59................................Guess Who?

60................................. Quiz Answers

62.... Where's our mascot, Mighty Red?

Welcome

The Liverpool FC Official 2013 Annual is packed full of features and interviews with your Anfield idols.

From new manager Brendan Rodgers to skipper Steven Gerrard and members of the first-team squad, we chat to the men who matter at LFC as they strive to bring the glory days back to the club.

We look back at last season which included an unforgettable Cup triumph, and there are quizzes to test your Kop knowledge as well as exclusive pictures to pin on your bedroom wall.

It's all in the Liverpool FC Official 2013 Annual.

SEASON REVIEW

August

Kenny Dalglish's Liverpool got their campaign underway with a 1-1 draw with Sunderland. Little did we know it by this early stage, but it was to prove to be the story of the season at home as domination failed to be turned into points as the Mackems cancelled out a Luis Suarez strike to salvage a point.

It was a much better start on the road, however, as Suarez was again on the mark as Liverpool recorded their first ever victory at Arsenal's Emirates Stadium, while the Carling Cup campaign got underway with a comfortable victory at Exeter as Andy Carroll struck his first goal of the campaign.

September

Two back to back defeats away from home proved costly in terms of the early league standings as Jon Walters netted the only goal of the game to give Stoke victory at the Britannia Stadium, and then in north London Tottenham went goal crazy to net four without reply as the Reds saw both Martin Skrtel and Charlie Adam sent off.

Spirits were lifted again though in the Carling Cup as Brighton were dispatched thanks to a Dirk Kuyt winner, and back at Anfield winning ways were resumed as Luis Suarez netted in a 2-1 victory over Wolves.

October

Andy Carroll was the darling of the red half of Merseyside with the opening and decisive goal in the Merseyside derby before Luis Suarez doubled the Liverpudlian joy and gave Kenny Dalglish yet another win in this famous fixture.

It was almost two memorable victories back to back after Steven Gerrard gave the home side the lead over Manchester United at Anfield, but the visitors struck ten minutes from time to save a point. Despite a late onslaught, which saw Jordan Henderson go close to snatching a winner, the Reds were once again left to rue missed chances at home.

It was the same story when Norwich City visited Merseyside as the Reds took the lead through Craig Bellamy only for the visitors to net against the run of play in the second half to deny Liverpool a deserved victory.

Again, solace was found in the Carling Cup as Luis Suarez netted twice to send Stoke crashing out of the competition and Liverpool through to the quarter finals.

November

Brendan Rodgers' Swansea City gave as impressive a display from an away side that Anfield saw all season as they battled to a well-deserved point in a goalless draw, much to the disappointment of the home fans who were by now becoming accustomed to seeing points slip away in front of their eyes.

Those supporters were celebrating wildly the following week, however, as Glen Johnson netted a glorious late winner to give the Reds victory at Chelsea.

Ironically, the Reds were back at Stamford Bridge again later in the month, this time for the Carling Cup quarter final, and it was the same story as Kenny Dalglish's side dominated the game and progressed to the last four thanks to goals from Maxi Rodriguez and Martin Kelly.

December

December is always regarded as a pivotal month in the footballing season, and the results for Liverpool perfectly summed up their season: very mixed.

A 1-0 defeat at Fulham was followed by a slender victory over QPR and then an impressive 2-0 success at Aston Villa was followed by disappointing back-to-back draws against Premier League strugglers Wigan and Blackburn.

The year ended on a high, however, as Steven Gerrard got amongst the goals in a 3-1 defeat of high-flying Newcastle at Anfield.

January

2011 may have ended well but 2012 started badly as Manchester City sent Liverpool crashing to a 3-0 defeat at the City of Manchester Stadium.

But the start of the FA Cup campaign quickly brought smiles back to Kopite faces as Oldham Athletic were sent packing in style, leaving Anfield on the back of a 5-1 defeat.

Two days later and the Reds were back at Manchester City for the first leg of the Carling Cup semi-final and turned in one of their finest displays of the campaign so far, with Steven Gerrard netting the only goal of the game from the penalty spot to give the Reds a first leg advantage.

The league troubles continued, however, as Stoke took a point away from Anfield in a goalless draw before relegation threatened Bolton smashed three into Pepe Reina's net to secure victory at the Reebok Stadium.

But when the bigger looking games came along it seemed the Reds regained their form and focus, and a 2-2 home draw with Manchester City in the second leg of the semi-final was enough to book Kenny Dalglish's men a place in the Carling Cup final. Craig Bellamy was the hero with a late goal to level the scores on the night and ensure Liverpool progressed on aggregate.

It proved to be a week to remember in the campaign as Manchester United were next up in the FA Cup and Dirk Kuyt struck late to send Anfield ecstasy as the fans celebrated their team enjoying another magical afternoon in the Cup competitions.

February

Points in the Barclays Premier League were still proving tough to pick up, though; as Tottenham held the Reds to a goalless draw on a Monday night at Anfield before a Wayne Rooney double secured a victory for Manchester United at Old Trafford.

The rest of the month was all about the Cups, however, and, true to form, the Reds kept up their impressive knock-out record with a thumping 6-1 FA Cup success over Brighton at Anfield before it was time to focus all eyes on the Carling Cup final.

Cardiff City were the opponents as Liverpool enjoyed their first ever visit to the new Wembley Stadium and despite kicking off the match as underdogs, the Championship side took a first half lead before Martin Skrtel restored parity with a second half strike. Substitute Dirk Kuyt then seemed to have snatched an extra time winner for the Reds, but it wasn't to be as the Bluebirds netted late on to force the agonising drama of a penalty shoot-out.

Ultimately it was Gerrard who cost his side the Cup – but thankfully not Steven Gerrard but rather his cousin Antony, who saw his spot-kick at sudden death roll past the post to give Liverpool their first major trophy in six years.

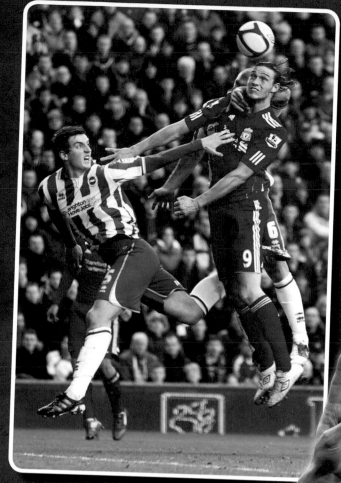

March

It was hoped Cup glory would be a springboard for improved fortunes and better results in the league, but those dreams were shattered by Robin van Persie, who struck an injury time winner for Arsenal at Anfield before Sunderland also took three points off the Reds at the Stadium of Light.

With a top four position looking more and more unlikely, it seemed as though the Reds would need more Cup success – this time in the FA Cup – if there was to be anything else for the fans to celebrate.

After a Steven Gerrard masterclass won the Anfield derby thanks to his stunning hat-trick, Stoke City were the next team to feel the force of the Reds in Cup competition as they were defeated 2-1.

But it was to be a terrible end to the month as Liverpool somehow squandered a 2-0 lead at QPR to lose 3-2 and then Wigan Athletic took all three points away from Anfield in an unlikely 2-1 victory which boosted their survival chances.

April

With the end of the season now in sight and the games coming thick and fast, April started badly for Liverpool as they went down 2-0 at Newcastle, leaving the gap between the two sides challenging for fourth more and more in the Geordies' favour.

A home draw with Aston Villa followed before spirits were restored ahead of the FA Cup semi-final showdown with Everton as Andy Carroll headed a late, late winner to secure a 3-2 victory at Blackburn.

And so then it was back to Wembley for the Merseyside derby showdown, with a place in the FA Cup final at stake.

It started badly for the Reds as the Blues struck first through Jelavic, but Luis Suarez was on hand in the second half to level the scores with a calm finish after charging through on goal. With time ticking away at the end of the game, Craig Bellamy floated a free kick into the area which was met by the head of Andy Carroll who glanced the ball home to book the Reds a place in the biggest domestic final in world football.

In keeping with the Reds' inconsistent season, however, the next match resulted in a home defeat to West Bromwich Albion before Luis Suarez netted a brilliant hat-trick to seal victory at Norwich.

May

Cup final month kicked off with a home loss to Fulham before it was time to turn attentions to the FA Cup final against Chelsea.

The Reds were looking to complete a domestic Cup double, but sadly didn't rise to the occasion for the first hour of the Wembley showpiece, allowing the Londoners to take control and take a 2-0 lead thanks to goals from Ramires and Drogba.

Andy Carroll came off the bench to give the Reds a lifeline with a well struck goal from close range, and although he had a claim for a second goal turned down when it looked as though the ball may have crossed the line, ultimately time ran out on Liverpool's hopes of celebrating more silverware.

With the final having come and gone there was little left to play for in the league. A 4-1 Anfield victory over Chelsea ensured some level of revenge for the Wembley disappointment, but in a season of up and down results it was no surprise that a thumping victory was followed in the final game of the campaign with a disappointing defeat at Swansea City – masterminded by Brendan Rodgers.

Brendan Rodgers

Brendan Rodgers is looking forward to the challenge of taking Liverpool back to the top of English football – but has stressed it may take time to realise all of our dreams.

The 39-year-old earned plenty of praise from neutrals for the style of play he implemented at Swansea, where flowing pass and move football made the Welsh side one of the easiest on the eye last term.

New boss Rodgers wants Liverpool to play a similar brand of football but he also accepts that it won't happen overnight. He said: "For me it is going to take time for how I want to play and the philosophy I want to introduce.

"My longer-term aim is to arrive here seeing how quickly we can do so.

"The principles of your game are based on the players you have and there is no doubt I'll have a look at that and see if there is anyone I need to bring in to improve that.

"We want to play winning football, effective football. I know what we need to play that way and win that way but ultimately that will be the job of the next period of time.

"It is about results and the progress of the team but we will make our first steps and hopefully that will improve over the next few years.

"What we need to do is improve the team and the quality of the team and hopefully over the next couple of years we will be ready to challenge and ready to compete."

For all the talk of how a Rodgers team will pass the ball, hard work and pressing opponents are just as important to the Northern Irishman.

"I hear people talking about working hard but for me it is an obligation - it's not a choice.

"We all work hard in our everyday lives as people and for players it is no different.

"It is quite simple. You come in and do a hard day's work. You make sure in training and on match days you come in and you can take your top off and wring it out and it will be soaking wet

"It is that honesty that you want. If you can work hard and you have got talent it takes you a long way.

"That will be the emphasis for me here - to try to reinforce that and ensure that commitment to the cause is important because we have a cause to fight for here."

Rodgers, who took over from Kenny Dalglish in the summer, also admits he's determined to align the brilliant support from the stands with quality on the pitch.

"I want to use the incredible support to make coming to Anfield the longest 90 minutes of an opponent's life," he added.

"I want to see great attacking football with creativity and imagination, with relentless passing of the ball.

"I know what it's like because I had a team like that at Swansea. That was with a terrific group of players. When people came to Swansea, it was probably the longest 90 minutes in their life. So after ten minutes, when they hadn't had a touch of the ball, they are looking at the clock and seeing only ten minutes had gone. It's a long afternoon.

"When you come to a club like this one, the shirt weighs much heavier than any other shirt," he said.

"The weight of expectation is phenomenal. My job next season is to try and lift some of that weight off the shirt. I'll take the pressure.

"The players can just go and concentrate on performing and if you don't do that you'll get the result eight or nine times out of ten because of your talent.

"The reality is that this is a club where I need to align the playing group with the supporters. There is an imbalance at the minute.

New Manager

"You've got some of the world's best supporters here and the playing group is not quite at that level yet. What excites me is the motivation to get that level back up again and that is why I came."

The pass and move philosophy which has become Liverpool's trademark is what Rodgers wants to bring to the pitch on a regular basis and he insists it is important to keep those traditions. He added: "I think every player will tell you they would love to play that way. The question is, does every player want to work that way?

"For me, a lot of our game is based on passing. Our game at Swansea was talked about a lot and lauded. What people didn't recognise is that to have the ball for 60-70 per cent of the game you have to get it back, very, very quickly.

"So our transition in the game and positioning to get the ball back became very good and that allowed us to beat Manchester City, to beat Arsenal, should have beaten Chelsea and to beat Liverpool.

"It's not starting from scratch but tweaking. I don't think it is a total rebuild.

"Obviously I have a philosophy in terms of where I want to get to but that won't happen on the first day. What we will need to do is make a number of adjustments and bring in players for key positions that will allow us to play that way.

"You can't come to Liverpool and play a direct game of football, lumping-it style.

"This is a club that is historic for the identity, style and DNA of its football."

Brendan Rodgers 15

Carling Cup Final
in Pictures

Carling Cup Final 17

YOU'LL NEVER WALK ALONE

LIVERPOOL
FOOTBALL CLUB

EST·1892

Steven Gerrard

Steven Gerrard is convinced Liverpool can lay claim to a top four place in this season's Barclays Premier League.

Despite a disappointing eighth place finish last term, the Reds' skipper believes Brendan Rodgers' attacking mindset will give the club a greater chance of achieving their aims this time around.

"I think we'll definitely see a much bolder Liverpool team this season and more exciting too, but with a quick transition to ensure we're organised when we lose the ball," he said.

"I think over the years sometimes Liverpool have come up against certain types of opposition and we have shown them too much respect. But maybe we have had to because of the style we've been asked to play.

"There were times under previous managers when we did that, but I think this manager is the opposite, he wants us to play like a big team.

"There's a lot of hard work and a lot of learning to be done sharpish if we want to implement that straight away. In only my second training session here, we were doing team shape and Brendan was telling players what he expects them to do movement wise, how he wants the team to do the transition when we lose the ball to win it back.

"I don't think a team has ever gone from eighth to first in one season but there are still other big targets for us to achieve – getting back into the top four is certainly the priority.

"I think we will get in the top four. I am confident we will get it. If we can play like we did in a lot of games last season, be clinical and take our chances, I think we will be high up in the table.

"The idea is to improve and have some fun along the way in the cup competitions like we did last year."

Gerrard has also challenged the club's galaxy of young stars – many of whom were given a chance to impress on the pre-season tour of North America – to seize their opportunity to shine.

"I see or hear some young lads talking about being patient or waiting for their chance," he says. "It sounds like they feel they need a 15-minute cameo in a first-team game to prove what they can do. That's not what it's about. It's about proving yourself every day in training.

"We train from 10am until 1pm or 2pm. In that time you have to show you don't want to wait around. Their attitude should be: it doesn't matter how old I am, I'm good enough. They don't want to be getting to September or October and wondering why they didn't get a chance in a game. 'Do it now', is my message to them.

"They have to go in every day and prove to the manager that they are better than those players who are in the team. Myself and Jamie and Michael didn't wait around on the fringes of the squad hoping we'd be selected some day. We showed on the training pitch that we would do whatever it took to make the boss put us in.

"We showed the mental strength required. We proved that we were as good as, if not better than, those who had been ahead of us. That's what these lads need to do."

Steven Gerrard 19

LIVERPOOL FC LEGENDS

ON THE NEW BOSS, BRENDAN RODGERS

" I saw Swansea in the play-offs last year and I saw them play against Liverpool this year and I've been very impressed with them. They play fantastic football, they really do. You look around now and it's amazing how many young managers there are in the game. That seems to be the thing now. It's a stressful game in the managers' position, so maybe the younger you are, the better! His job will be to get Liverpool up there and the aim is to win the Premier League. You ask any Liverpool fan - that's the number one aim. **"**

Ian Callaghan

" When I joined Liverpool, it was all about pass and move. You would pass all the time, keep possession, and try not to give the ball away. It was all you were told to do and far too often over the past 10 years or so, Liverpool have given the ball away far too cheaply. I think Swansea City and Brendan Rodgers were a breath of fresh air last year and if he can bring that to Liverpool and win a lot of games and bring what we all want – top European football to the table, he'll be a King around the place. You've got to start somewhere; he is a young manager and he's very, very gifted. Hopefully this is the right time and the right place for the man. **"**

John Aldridge

" As far as I am concerned Brendan Rodgers is an outstanding young manager. I think he plays in a very modern and comprehensive way and you can see what he has done at Swansea. I always say that when you have a philosophy on football, you need the players who can instil that. **"**

John Barnes

" Brendan Rodgers' philosophy on football is a good one, he always wants to see his sides play football and that's how Liverpool fans want their team to play. **"**

David Fairclough

" He has got a great pedigree. He has been in the game for nigh on 20 years and he's learnt a lot from the likes of Mourinho, Van Gaal and one or two other quality coaches as well. He is the best choice for the job. He is a quality choice, there is no doubt about it. I think he understands what the club is all about and what the fans mean to the club as well. That is very, very important. I think the players will relish working with a guy who knows the game inside out. **"**

Alan Kennedy

> " He wants his teams to pass in all areas. He has used a system that has worked in Spain, especially for Barcelona – principally the two centre halves split, the full backs push on and the holding midfielder steps in and plays from there. Everyone is encouraged to get on the ball, take risks, pass it, keep it. Liverpool will be playing the tiki-taka style. This squad should be excited about working with Brendan because he won't waste a training session, where he will be working with the ball and teaching them how to break down other teams. "

Jamie Redknapp

> " When he was in the running for the job, one of the candidates, I was speaking to the Chelsea boys and some of the players that have experienced working with him as well. They all spoke really highly of him. They said he's a good coach, a good guy, very honest and he supports his players very well. That's all you ask for as a player, we're really looking forward to it. I'm excited. I'm really looking forward to working with Brendan. We shared a phone call last night and I'm really looking forward to meeting him in person and getting started working with him. "

Steven Gerrard

> " Congratulations to Brendan and Good Luck to everyone at LFC. "

Kenny Dalglish

> " He's done a fantastic job and exceeded all expectations. He's most probably one of the managers of the season because of the football that Swansea play. It's no surprise Swansea have done so well because they've always played great football. Brendan has just taken them to the next level. They've exceeded many people's expectations. "

Ian Rush

> " For what Brendan Rodgers has achieved at Swansea, he deserves huge respect. He's worked under José Mourinho at Chelsea so he knows the score and he's worked with top players. It will be a massive step-up for Rodgers to manage Liverpool. "

Robbie Fowler

Jordan Henderson

Jordan Henderson reflects on his first season at Liverpool, admitting the time he has spent on Merseyside since signing from Sunderland has been punctuated by both highs and lows.

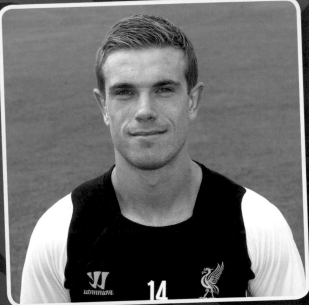

The 21-year-old was proud to have started in three Wembley outings in the space of just four months in 2012 and is delighted that the Reds were able to end a six-year wait for silverware by winning the Carling Cup in February this year.

However, the youngster also knows he and his teammates are capable of performing to higher standards in the league and insists there has been ample evidence throughout last year's campaign to indicate the team's potential to climb the table next year.

"Overall, it's been an up and down season," Henderson said. "But I think we have achieved great things as a team in winning the Carling Cup and getting to the final of the FA Cup.

"They are two big achievements and winning the Carling Cup was a great achievement for the club because it meant we got back to winning trophies. But we know our league form will need to improve for next year.

"We are well aware of that and I'm sure that we'll work on that and we'll get better at it. I think there are positive signs there that we can do that. We have hit the post and the bar a lot of times this season so we need to be more clinical in front of goal and a bit more streetwise as well.

"We've got a lot to learn but if we can do that and rectify the mistakes we've made this season then we can definitely be better equipped to improve next year.

"I've played in a lot of different positions throughout the course of this season but I don't think that's an excuse."

Henderson took part in 37 of the 38 Premier League games during his debut season at Anfield and the youngster, who played 71 games for Sunderland before making the switch to Merseyside, is delighted to have featured so prominently during his first campaign.

"That's been very pleasing," said Henderson. "Obviously I want to play in every game that I'm fit and available for, so yes, I've enjoyed playing on a regular basis and hopefully I can carry on doing that.

"That gelling process doesn't just happen overnight but I think good players should be able to play with each other pretty quickly. It depends which way you look at it but, of course, it takes time for everyone to gel."

Henderson's performances earned him a call-up to the England squad for the European Championships when Frank Lampard was ruled out with injury, much to the delight of his club and international skipper Steven Gerrard.

"Jordan is a very exciting player, one for the future, and it is a great opportunity for him," said Gerrard.

'"What people have got to understand is that he is still very young in football terms.

'He is 21, he will gain experience, he will gain confidence, he will gain belief and he will improve and get stronger.

'I was 21 and was nowhere near the finished article."

Jordan Henderson 23

Joe Allen

Liverpool's Welsh wonder Joe Allen is looking forward to continuing his footballing education under Brendan Rodgers – and has tipped the new-look Reds to bring the glory days back to Anfield.

Having linked up with Rodgers at Swansea, Allen didn't need to think twice when the new Liverpool manager gave him the opportunity of a summer move to Merseyside.

"Look at the players and staff, and obviously the supporters, and everything is there for us to be successful," said the Wales international.

"I'm looking forward to being part of some great years ahead for Liverpool Football Club.

"I have a lot of faith that Brendan Rodgers can bring success, that's one of the reasons I'm here. I wanted to be part of this project, his project, and I've really got a good feeling - as I'm sure all the players here have - that this football club is going to go from strength to strength in the next couple of seasons

"Brendan is so passionate about his football. He works day in, day out to improve the team and everyone individually. Everyone wants to work alongside someone who has that way about them.

"One of his best things is his man management, it's second to none. He commands the respect of everyone and it's no different for me.

"To join back up with him was definitely a big pull for me."

He added: "It was hard to believe at first and very flattering to be linked to a top club like this. It shows you're doing something right, I guess.

"I've always been ambitious and wanting to get to the top but getting there is a completely different thing. It's definitely hard to believe. It's been a quick rise for me."

Allen is now looking forward to plying his trade at Anfield – and admits to a sense of excitement about turning out in the red shirt

"The whole atmosphere at this ground is very rare," he said. "The passion that people here have for football is something I share and I want to be part of that. It's another part of the pull to this great club.

"As a Swansea player, that was one of the days you really remembered from last season. To get the chance to be here and have that as my home ground is a special feeling.

"I can't wait to experience the famous Liverpool support.

"I can't really imagine how I'll feel playing at Anfield right now. I'm excited about that prospect and witnessing the Anfield atmosphere and spirit, and being part of the home team, I'm sure it will be incredible.

"It's an opportunity for me personally. I've always been ambitious and wanted to play at the highest level I possibly could. When you see an opportunity like this it's almost impossible to turn it down.

"I'm someone who wants to be the best I can be. Every day, in training or in matches, I always want to improve. You'll always get 100 per cent out of me and I'm really looking forward to gelling with the top-class players who are here and doing my bit for the club.

"I feel proud, I'm really thrilled and I'm looking forward to my time here."

His new boss is thrilled at the prospect, too, and insists his young midfielder will fit perfectly into his vision for the future.

"This boy, when you see him play, you would think he was a European player," said Rodgers. "He is a unique player in that he is a British player who doesn't give the ball away.

"He's incredible on the ball. His body work and

New Signing

"You will see when he comes into this team the difference he can make. His game understanding is very good, and he is in love with the football.

"He wants the ball all the time, and he has so much courage to get on the ball and play. I think he will fit in really well with all the other clever players we have at the club."

Joe Allen 25

José Enrique

José Enrique has spoken of his desire to lift more trophies with Liverpool after tasting Carling Cup success last season.

The Reds' full back – who is starting his second full season with the club – has also outlined his desire to force his way into Spain's all-conquering national team after watching his international teammates celebrate Euro 2012 glory in the summer.

"Last year I won a title (Carling Cup) and it was amazing with the fans here, I enjoyed it a lot. This season I hope we can win something again and try to play for the Champions League," he said.

The mood in the Liverpool camp has been buoyed by the arrival of Brendan Rodgers as boss – and Enrique has also admitted to being more than pleased with what he's seen so far.

"I am really happy," Enrique added. "For me it is the best way to play football, like Spain did, that's why they are the best at the moment.

"With the manager we play with the ball a lot and we are really happy with him.

"I'm really impressed. I know how he likes to play because we played against Swansea last year and I've seen them many times.

"He has only had a short time with us but the training has been great. He is talking to both the young and experienced players the same, and I love that because it is really important to have the same treatment for both.

"The training is all with the ball, what more do you want? It's really hard, but it's very good. We have good players here to play in this way, and I think this season we can impress."

Enrique also revealed his 'dream' of playing for the Spanish team which won Euro 2012 – although he appreciates the fight he has on his hands to claim a place.

"I watched all the games, they were amazing. Football is about moments – and now it is Spain's," he said. "Before it was Brazil and Argentina. Spain try to play this way now and I think this is the best way to play. They've won many titles together now, and I'm really happy to be Spanish!

"To be in the national team is the best for a footballer. To be in a team like Spain is a dream for me. I know it's really hard now because Jordi Alba played in the Euros and did very well and he has just signed for Barcelona.

"I'm still working to be there in the future. If I can be there, of course it would be a dream, but my job is here to play for Liverpool and there are still many things to do here."

José Enrique 27

120
MEMORABLE MOMENTS

Liverpool FC celebrated its 120th birthday in 2012 – and so we've put together a list of 120 milestone moments from the club's history.

2. The new club play their first competitive match and mark the occasion with an 8-0 rout of Higher Walton in the Lancashire League (September 1892)

1. Liverpool Football Club is officially born, with John Houlding its founding chairman (June 1892)

9. The title returns to Anfield as the Reds finish the season four points ahead of nearest challengers Preston (April 1906)

10. Legendary goalkeeper Elisha Scott makes his senior Liverpool debut and keeps a clean sheet in a goalless draw away at Newcastle (January 1913)

11. The Reds reach the FA Cup Final for the first time but lose 1-0 to Burnley at Crystal Palace (April 1914)

12. Liverpool embark on their first foreign tour with a five-game end-of-season trip to Scandinavia (May 1914)

3. Liverpool are elected to the Football League Division Two and get off to a winning start with a 2-0 victory away to Middlesbrough Ironopolis (September 1893)

4. Promotion to the top-flight is secured at the first attempt courtesy of a 2-0 Test Match success against Newton Heath (April 1894)

5. The Reds record what remains their highest-ever victory in League football as Rotherham Town are pummelled 10-1 at Anfield (February 1896)

6. The club's first superstar player Alex Raisbeck joins the club for £350 from Stoke City (May 1898)

7. The highly-regarded Tom Watson is recruited from Sunderland as secretary-manager (August 1896)

8. Liverpool are crowned champions of England for the first time (April 1901)

13. The First Division Championship is clinched for a third time following a 2-1 home defeat of Burnley (April 1922)

14. Liverpool complete back-to-back title triumphs (May 1923)

15. The first ever foreign player is signed when South African goalkeeper Arthur Riley arrives from Boksburg FC (August 1925)

16. A roof is put on the Spion Kop, making it one of the most atmospheric terraces in world football (August 1928)

22. Jack Balmer creates history by scoring three consecutive hat-tricks (November 1946)

23. Liverpool are confirmed as the inaugural post-war champions after Stoke fail to defeat Sheffield United in their final league game of an extended season (June 1947)

24. Liverpool's first visit to Wembley ends in disappointment as Arsenal run out 2-0 winners to take the FA Cup (April 1950)

25. Anfield's all-time record attendance of 61,905 is set when Wolves visit for a FA Cup fourth round tie (February 1952)

26. Liverpool suffer the indignity of relegation from the top-flight for the third time in their history after finishing bottom of the pile with just 28 points (April 1954)

27. Liverpool endure their heaviest-ever defeat at St Andrews as Birmingham City romp to an emphatic 9-1 success (December 1954)

28. Second Division Liverpool cause the shock of the FA Cup 4th round with a resounding 4-0 victory over their top-flight Mersey neighbours Everton at Goodison Park (January 1955)

29. The floodlights are switched on at Anfield for the first time as the Reds host Everton in a friendly to commemorate the 75th anniversary of the Liverpool County FA (October 1957)

30. Liverpool suffer their most humiliating-ever defeat in the third round of the FA Cup to non-league Worcester City (January 1959)

17. Gordon Hodgson registers his club record 17th and final hat-trick in a Liverpool shirt (February 1935)

18. Liverpool beat Everton 6-0 at Anfield in what is still their best-ever derby win (September 1935)

19. Jack Balmer scores what is genuinely regarded as the quickest-ever Liverpool goal when he nets after just ten seconds of the 3-1 derby win at Goodison (February 1938)

20. Albert Stubbins joins the Reds in a record-breaking transfer deal from Newcastle United (September 1946)

21. Billy Liddell scores his first competitive Liverpool goal as the Reds come out on top in a sensational eleven goal Anfield thriller against Chelsea (September 1946)

31. Bill Shankly is appointed as Phil Taylor's successor as manager at Anfield (December 1959)

32. All-time record appearance holder Ian Callaghan makes his Liverpool debut and stars in a 4-1 Anfield win over Bristol Rovers (April 1959)

33. Liverpool smash their transfer record by forking out £37,500 to capture Motherwell forward Ian St John (May 1961)

34. A Kevin Lewis double in a 2-0 home win over Southampton confirms promotion, ending Liverpool's eight-year exile in Division Two (April 1962)

35. You'll Never Walk Alone tops the British music charts and is adopted as the Kop's unofficial anthem (October 1963)

36. Liverpool play in European competition for the first team and mark the occasion with a 5-0 rout of Reykjavik in Iceland (August 1964)

37. Anfield is the setting for the first ever Match of the Day as the Reds host Arsenal on the opening day of the season (August 1964)

38. Liverpool sport their now famous all-red strip for the first time in a European Cup tie at home to Anderlecht (November 1964)

39. The FA Cup is won for the first time as Leeds United are beaten on a historic afternoon at Wembley (May 1965)

40. Liverpool reclaim their mantle as English champions following a 2-1 home win over Chelsea (April 1966)

41. In their first-ever European Final the Reds lose to 2-1 to Borussia Dortmund at Hampden Park (May 1966)

42. Champions Liverpool win the Charity Shield outright for the first time courtesy of a 1-0 win over FA Cup winners Everton at Goodison (August 1966)

43. Kevin Keegan scores in front of the Kop on his debut as Liverpool record an opening day 3-1 success against Nottingham Forest (August 1971)

44. Liverpool win a record-equalling 8th league title (May 1973)

45. Europe is conquered for the first time as Borussia Moenchengladbach are beaten over two legs in the final of the UEFA Cup (May 1973)

46. Liverpool win the FA Cup for a second time following a comprehensive 3-0 thrashing of Newcastle at Wembley (May 1974)

47. Bill Shankly sensationally announces his resignation as Liverpool manager (July 1974)

48. Bob Paisley reluctantly accepts to take over the Anfield managerial reigns (July 1974)

49. Liverpool chalk up their best ever victory with an 11-0 rout of Stromsgodset Drammen in a first round European Cup Winners Cup tie at Anfield (September 1974)

50. A thrilling 3-1 victory over Wolves at Molineux clinches a 9th Championship success (May 1976)

51. FC Bruges are beaten over two legs as the UEFA Cup is won for a second time (May 1976)

52. David Fairclough scores one of Anfield's most celebrated goals as French champions St Etienne are famously defeated in the European Cup quarter-final (March 1977)

53. A goalless draw at home to West Ham is enough to secure a 10th League crown for the Reds (May 1977)

54. Liverpool beat Borussia Moenchengladbach 3-1 in Rome to win the European Cup for the first time (May 1977)

55. Kenny Dalglish joins Liverpool for a British record £440,000 from Celtic (August 1977)

56. Kevin Keegan returns to Anfield with Hamburg but finds himself on the wrong end of Terry McDermott-inspired 6-0 rout that secures the European Super Cup for a first time (December 1977)

57. Liverpool reach the League Cup Final for the first time but, following a goalless draw at Wembley, they are defeated 1-0 by Nottingham Forest in an Old Trafford replay (March 1978)

58. Liverpool become the first English club to retain the European Cup courtesy of a 1-0 victory over FC Bruges at Wembley (May 1978)

59. A 3-0 Anfield victory over Aston Villa confirms Liverpool 11th League title (May 1979)

60. Avi Cohen scores for both teams as Liverpool best Aston Villa 4-1 at Anfield to clinch a 12th First Division title (May 1980)

61. Liverpool bury their League Cup hoodoo with a 2-1 victory over West Ham in a replayed final at Villa Park (April 1981)

62. Howard Gayle becomes the first Liverpool substitute to be substituted but only after running amok in Munich's Olympic Stadium as the Reds eliminate Bayern on away goals in the European Cup semi-final (April 1981)

63. Alan Kennedy is the unlikely goalscoring hero as Liverpool defeat Real Madrid 1-0 in Paris to win a third European Cup (May 1981)

64. Liverpool set a new club transfer record to sign Brighton & Hove Albion defender Mark Lawrenson for £900,000 (August 1981)

65. Liverpool Football Club's modern day founding father Bill Shankly passes away (September 1981)

66. Goals from Ronnie Whelan (2) and Ian Rush see Liverpool come from behind to retain the League Cup with a 3-1 victory over Tottenham at Wembley (March 1982)

67. Liverpool celebrate a 13th title triumph in front of the Kop as Spurs are beaten 3-1 on the final Saturday of the season (May 1982)

71. Liverpool and Everton compete in the first all-Merseyside Wembley final but it takes a solitary Graeme Souness strike in the Maine Road replay to decide the destiny of the Milk Cup (March 1984)

72. A goalless draw against Notts County at Meadow Lane is enough to confirm a 15th League Championship triumph (May 1984)

73. Alan Kennedy's successful penalty conversion clinches a dramatic shoot-out victory over AS Roma in Rome and a fourth European Cup for the club (May 1984)

74. A grief-stricken Joe Fagan steps down as Liverpool boss after the Heysel Stadium disaster, in which 39 fans are killed prior to the European Cup Final defeat by Juventus (May 1985)

68. Bob Paisley becomes the first manager to go up the steps at Wembley and collect a trophy as Liverpool win the League (Milk) Cup for a third successive season courtesy of a 2-1 win after extra-time in the final against Manchester United (March 1983)

69. Bob Paisley bows out as Liverpool manager after leading the Reds to a 14th First Division title (May 1983)

70. Backroom stalwart Joe Fagan succeeds Paisley as manager (June 1983)

75. Liverpool achieve the coveted League and FA Cup double. Player/boss Kenny Dalglish scores the only goal of the game to clinch the title at Stamford Bridge and the following week Everton are beaten in the Cup Final at Wembley (May 1986)

76. Club record goalscorer Ian Rush signs off with a goal v Watford on his last Anfield appearance before joining Juventus (May 1987)

77. John Barnes becomes the first black player to sign for Liverpool when he completes his £900,000 switch from Watford (June 1987)

84. A last-gasp Michael Thomas strike denies Liverpool a second double and secures the title for Arsenal on a dramatic night at Anfield (May 1989)

85. A 2-1 home win against Queens Park Rangers sees Liverpool clinch an 18th League Championship (April 1990)

86. Kenny Dalglish sensationally announces that he's stepping down as Liverpool manager (February 1991)

78. Liverpool break their transfer record to capture the signature of Newcastle United's Peter Beardsley, paying the Geordies £1.9 million (July 1987)

79. After going 29 games unbeaten from the start of the season, a 1-0 home win over Tottenham confirms a 17th League Championship triumph (April 1988)

80. John Aldridge becomes the first player to miss a penalty in the FA Cup Final as the Reds are surprisingly defeated 1-0 at Wembley by Wimbledon, quashing dreams of a second double (May 1988)

81. After just one season with Juventus, Ian Rush re-signs for the Reds (August 1988)

82. 96 Liverpool fans are tragically killed at Hillsborough as a result of crushing on the Leppings Lane terrace at the start of the FA Cup semi-final against Nottingham Forest (April 1989)

87. Former skipper Graeme Souness is unveiled as Liverpool manager (April 1991)

88. Michael Thomas and Ian Rush are on the scoresheet as Liverpool beat Sunderland 2-0 at Wembley to win the FA Cup for a 5th time (May 1992)

89. Ian Rush becomes the club's all-time record goalscorer (October 1992)

90. Teenage striking sensation Robbie Fowler nets five times on his Anfield debut in a League Cup tie against Fulham (October 1993)

83. Ian Rush comes off the bench to net twice as Liverpool defeat Everton 3-2 in an emotionally-charged FA Cup Final at Wembley (May 1989)

91. A shock 1-0 home defeat to Bristol City in an FA Cup third round replay is the prelude to Graeme Souness stepping down from his post as Reds boss (January 1994)

92. Boot-room boy Roy Evans replaces Souness as Liverpool manager (January 1994)

93. Fans stand on the Kop for a final time before it's demolished to make way for an all-seater grandstand (April 1994)

94. Robbie Fowler scores the fastest hat-trick in Premier League history as Liverpool defeat Arsenal 3-0 at Anfield (August 1994)

95. A Steve McManaman double inspires Liverpool to victory over Bolton Wanderers in the Coca-Cola Cup Final at Wembley (April 1995)

96. Inspired by a young Michael Owen and Jamie Carragher, Liverpool win the FA Youth Cup for a first time with a two-legged triumph over West Ham (May 1996)

97. Michael Owen makes his senior debut against Wimbledon at Selhurst Park and nets to become the club's youngest ever goalscorer (May 1997)

98. In a ground-breaking move by the club Frenchman Gerard Houllier is appointed joint-manager of the Reds alongside Roy Evans (July 1998)

99. Liverpool celebrate their first appearance at Cardiff's Millennium Stadium by defeating Birmingham City on penalties to win the Worthington Cup (February 2001)

100. Michael Owen snatches the FA Cup from Arsenal's grasp with a late brace of goals as Liverpool come from behind to win 2-1 at the Millennium Stadium in Cardiff (May 2001)

101. On a thrilling night in Dortmund Liverpool complete an unprecedented cup treble with a thrilling 5-4 victory over Alaves in the greatest UEFA Cup Final of all-time (May 2001)

102. Michael Owen becomes the first Liverpool player to win the coveted Ballon D'Or (European Footballer of the Year) (December 2001)

103. Goals from Steven Gerrard and Michael Owen seal a 2-0 Worthington Cup Final success over Manchester United in Cardiff (March 2003)

104. Rafael Benitez is unveiled as the new Reds boss (June 2004)

105. Liverpool stage the most heroic ever comeback to win the Champions League on penalties after trailing AC Milan 3-0 at the interval in Istanbul (May 2005)

106. In one of the most exciting FA Cup Finals of all time, Liverpool fight back to 3-3 against West Ham before taking the cup on penalties (May 2006)

119. Steven Gerrard becomes the first Liverpool player since Ian Rush to score a hat-trick in the Merseyside derby (March 2012)

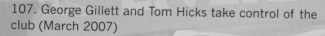

107. George Gillett and Tom Hicks take control of the club (March 2007)

108. Liverpool compete in their seventh European Cup Final but a brace of goals from Pippo Inzaghi condemns them to a 2-1 defeat in Athens (May 2007)

109. Club record signing Fernando Torres marks his Anfield debut with a goal of sublime class in a 1-1 draw with Chelsea (August 2007)

110. Jack Robinson, at 16 years and 250 days old, becomes Liverpool's youngster-ever player when coming on as a second-half substitute in the final Premier League game of the season away to Hull City (May 2010)

111. The managerial reign of Rafa Benitez comes to an end by mutual consent (June 2010)

112. Fulham boss Roy Hodgson is unveiled as Liverpool's 18th manager (July 2010)

113. Following a dramatic courtroom battle New England Sports Ventures (NESV) end months of uncertainty by completing their purchase of the club (October 2011)

114. Roy Hodgson's brief spell at the Anfield helm is brought to an end in the wake of a morale-shattering defeat away to Blackburn Rovers (January 2011)

115. Kenny Dalglish returns for his second stint as Liverpool manager (January 2011)

116. A dramatic transfer deadline day sees two club records smashed as Fernando Torres leaves for Chelsea and Andy Carroll signs from Newcastle (January 2011)

117. Luis Suarez comes off the bench to score on his Liverpool debut at home to Stoke City (February 2011)

118. On their first visit to the new Wembley Liverpool defeat Cardiff City on penalties to win the Carling Cup, the club's eighth triumph in the competition (February 2012)

120. After the club parts company with Kenny Dalglish in May, Brendan Rodgers is appointed Liverpool manager (June 2012)

YOU'LL NEVER WALK ALONE

LIVERPOOL
FOOTBALL CLUB

EST·1892

Martin Skrtel

Martin Skrtel admits Liverpool were frustrated with their league performance last term – but insists there are aspects of the campaign that can provide the basis for a much more fruitful 2012-13 campaign.

The centre-back, who was voted as LFC's Standard Chartered Player of the Season, believes the Reds can take positives from their overall standard of displays against teams from the top four in addition to their performances in the cup competitions.

Skrtel said: "The positives are the games against United, City, Chelsea or Arsenal. I think the performances of the team were good in these games.

"If you look at the game against City at Anfield, we played much, much better than them. We created so, so many chances but we couldn't get the three points.

"That was a game against a big team and the performance was good, but in the games against teams from the bottom half of the table were not too good. If were thinking about positives, they have to be performances against teams in the top four.

"I think we can build on it and if we can repeat the performances we gave against the teams in the top four and score more goals than we did this season, it can be good."

Liverpool finished the Barclays Premier League season in eighth position with 52 points, though they did win the Carling Cup and reach the final of the FA Cup.

"Especially in the league, everybody knows it wasn't a great season because we finished in eighth position and that's not good," said Skrtel.

"I think we deserved to finish higher than eighth position, but there were too many games in which we didn't get three points - and there were too many games in which we didn't get what we deserved.

"In the games at Anfield, I think we did well and created a lot of chances, but we couldn't take them and didn't get three points.

"We won the Carling Cup and got to the final of the FA Cup, so from that point of view it was a good season in the cups - but I think the most important thing is the league and we didn't get enough in it."

After winning the Carling Cup against Cardiff City at Wembley in February, Liverpool ended a six-year wait for silverware.

Skrtel added: "That was important for us because Liverpool hadn't won a trophy for a while, but we managed to do it in the Carling Cup and we also tried to win the FA Cup.

"We won a trophy, and we can be happy about that."

On a personal level, Skrtel enjoyed an impressive season culminating in him being voted as the clear winner in the club's Player of the Season poll.

"I got an injury in pre-season and missed the first two games, but I think the game against Bolton helped me when I came on as a sub for Kells (Martin Kelly) and scored a goal," reflected Skrtel.

"That was very important for me and I got confidence from it.

"From a personal point of view, I think my performances were alright - but the most important thing is the team. The team didn't do well and that is disappointing for me."

So apart from landing the fans' top award, what was his highlight of the campaign?

"I think the goal in the Carling Cup final was my highlight of the season because we were losing 1-0. I scored to make it 1-1 and helped the team to win the trophy, he said.

"I scored more goals, so that is the main thing. In the past I didn't score too many goals, but this season I scored four. I think that's not bad for a defender.

"If I look at my game, I think I played more aggressive than I did last season or the one before that.

"That's good because a defender has to be aggressive, so I have tried to improve on it and I think I did."

Martin Skrtel 37

CROSSWORD

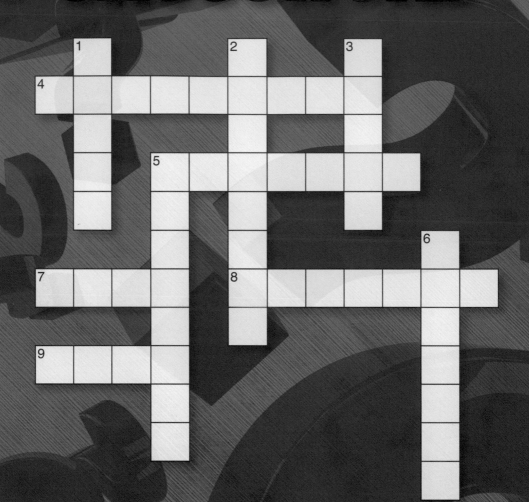

ACROSS

4 Jose Enrique signed for the Reds from which club? (9)

5 Brendan Rodgers arrived at Liverpool from which club? (7)

7 Which ex-Red left the club for Fenerbahce in the summer? (4)

8 Which country does Luis Suarez represent? (7)

9 From which club did Liverpool sign Fabio Borini? (4))

DOWN

1 Which Liverpool player was part of Spain's Euro 2012 winning squad? (5)

2 Liverpool won their fifth European Cup in which city? (8)

3 Kenny Dalglish wore which famous number at Anfield? (5)

5 Charlie Adam plays for which international team? (8)

6 Designer of Liverpool's 2012/13 kit. (7)

Answers on Page 60

WORDSEARCH

Take a look at the grid below and see if you can find 12 Liverpool related words. Words can go horizontally, vertically and diagonally in all eight directions.

Y	L	K	N	A	H	S	I	R	G	P
N	J	G	K	P	N	S	J	O	E	D
H	N	F	T	R	T	I	R	I	R	K
S	N	M	O	A	T	Z	E	R	R	M
I	Y	T	N	W	E	D	H	R	A	J
L	K	B	Y	R	L	P	G	A	R	N
G	U	J	A	E	L	E	A	W	D	G
L	P	U	I	L	B	O	R	I	N	I
A	S	F	P	O	K	P	R	R	Y	D
D	N	X	K	D	B	M	A	R	K	R
A	M	C	T	L	T	Y	C	D	Z	F

Anfield	Dalglish	Istanbul	Shankly
Borini	Fowler	Kop	Suarez
Carragher	Gerrard	Reina	Warrior

Answers on Page 60

Martin Kelly

Martin Kelly looked ahead to a brand new future under Brendan Rodgers and admitted 'These are exciting times'.

The Reds' youngster is enjoying proving himself under a new boss and is confident good times lie ahead for the club.

"The training sessions have been enjoyable and it's total football," said Kelly.

"It's hard on the fitness but after the session you really feel as though you have benefited from it and in the long term I think everyone will benefit from this style of play.

"This style suits my game, whether I'm playing centre-half or right-back, and everyone is excited for the new season.

"It's a positive way to play and everyone is enjoying it. I think any fan who has seen the squad train will be really excited about the new season."

Kelly once again faces a fight to claim a place in the side, up against the challenges coming from both Glen Johnson and Jon Flanagan.

But after being called up to the England squad for Euro 2012, Kelly's confidence is high as he looks to further his impressive young career to date.

He added: "It was a really positive experience for me to go away with England and it was a massive privilege for me to go away with such quality players.

"They accepted me so quickly and the other Liverpool players helped me feel right at home. I took a lot from those four weeks.

"We did a lot of defensive work and I definitely learned more about positional play, and because of that experience I've settled back into training quicker than I usually do.

"I'm always eager to impress. I tried to impress the past managers at this club and it's the same again with the new manager. I know my opportunity will come again and when I get the chance I want to impress as much as possible.

"It's great to be back with the lads and getting to work with the new manager. We have had our break now, we love our football and can't wait to get started."

Martin Kelly 41

Raheem Sterling

Liverpool youngster Raheem Sterling believes the new training methods introduced by manager Brendan Rodgers will help the Reds achieve success this term.

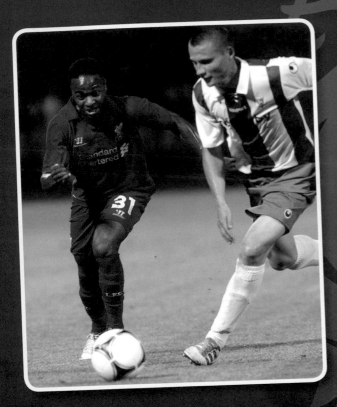

Sterling, whose talents have excited fans at youth and reserve team levels over the past couple of seasons, insists the emphasis on ball work (as opposed to long endurance sessions) has met with approval from the first team squad at Melwood.

"The training has been more enjoyable than other seasons because it has been more ball-related," he said. "That's definitely been a surprise - I was expecting long hill runs but it's nice to come in and do ball work.

"The manager is getting us to play football. You can see improvement in the movement of the ball - it's been really good football so far.

"Everyone is buzzing and they're loving the training. All the young lads are saying they love the way things are going and we are really enjoying it.

"The manager makes everyone feel welcome, even the young lads who are coming up. For him to speak to us is really good. He's given us advice, he's a good manager."

Sterling made his debut for the Reds when he appeared as a late substitute against Wigan at Anfield back in March – and he admits it's a moment he'll never forget.

"It was a shock to be in the squad," admitted Sterling. "But it was really exciting for me and when Dalglish said my name, I was like: 'Me? Are you sure?'

"So I put my shirt on and it just didn't feel real. It felt like I was dreaming and when I got on the pitch, I got caught up in the atmosphere of the stadium. It was one of the best experiences of my whole life.

"I was just thinking 'something I've dreamt about all my life is about to come true' and to finally get the chance to come on and play for a club like Liverpool was great. I was a bit nervous but once I got on the pitch and got my first touch of the ball, I relaxed a bit and it was really enjoyable.

"On the pitch, the players are always speaking to you to make you feel as though you are part of the team which is good. I was shouted at a few times, but you just have to deal with that!

He added: "After it, people congratulated me and it was nice knowing all the fans really wanted to see me play. After that I would get recognised a bit more. The first time I got asked (for an autograph), I had to check they meant me! But after that you get used to it.

"My mum keeps me grounded though; she lets me know what is right and wrong. She was really happy when I made my debut. My whole family has moved up here, so as much as it is me doing it on the pitch, she helps me off the pitch, so I have to thank her. She's a really helpful person in my life.

"The people at the Academy made me feel very welcome and the football that they have brought to the Academy, I've got to say, is really, really top quality. So I've got to say thank you to them for being there and helping me out with everything over the past few years. I'm really thankful for that."

Raheem Sterling 43

Nuri Sahin

Nuri Sahin has revealed how Kop favourite Xabi Alonso was instrumental in him agreeing a one-year loan deal with the Reds.

Sahin has agreed to spend this season working under Brendan Rodgers at Liverpool – and believes there's no reason why Reds' fans can't look forward to a year of success.

"The style the team is playing is very good and, of course, Liverpool has to play in the Champions League," Sahin said.

"A big club like Liverpool has to play every year in the Champions League and we will do everything to get in the top four.

"Also there is the FA Cup, League Cup and Europa League, and with the potential we have here, we can do some good things.

"The project with Liverpool and Brendan Rodgers is the best for my situation I think - that is why I am here.

"I think the style I play is the same as how the manager wants the team to play. We've had a lot of conversations. We spoke and he told me about his ideas for how he wants to play football and where he sees me on the field for the team. I was impressed with how much he loves football.

"He told me about how he wants to play football and what the goals are he wants to reach with Liverpool.

"I have settled in very well and I hope it will be the same on the pitch and that we will have a great season."

Liverpool beat off stiff competition in the race for Sahin's signature – and the Reds have a former hero to thank for helping to sell the advantages of a move to Merseyside.

"Xabi (Alonso) is a person who really cares about football. He's in love with football. I'm the same, and that's why we had a lot of conversations," he said. "When I arrived at Real Madrid, we spoke about German football and Italian football. He loves football. When he heard Liverpool were interested in me he started telling me about the club. He's still in love with Liverpool Football Club, I think.

New Signing

"It's crazy how he was telling me about Liverpool. He was saying 'go there, you'll love it. The fans will take care of you and love you'. He said Anfield is the best stadium in the world. Xabi won a lot of trophies here, and hopefully we can too."

Madrid boss Jose Mourinho also played his part in convincing the young midfielder he would be making the right decision to sign for the Reds.

"Jose told me that English football, especially the Premier League, is the best to enjoy as a footballer. Every weekend you can enjoy football. He also told me about how he and Brendan Rodgers worked together at Chelsea and that he's a good coach and person. That's important for me. It's not only football, it was very important for me to have someone I can speak with.

"I want to play football – and it was important for me to be at a club where the manager really wants me. I wanted to play for a club on the same level as Dortmund or Madrid – that's why I chose Liverpool. This year, it is very important for me to play. I have to play, improve my game and help the team. If I stay in good condition I am sure I can help the team and Liverpool FC, and Brendan Rodgers and the team can help me."

Fabio Borini

Italian international Fabio Borini became Brendan Rodgers' first signing as Liverpool manager when he arrived from AS Roma in July. Shortly after putting pen to paper on his Anfield deal he spoke to the club's official website...

Fabio, how does it feel to be a Liverpool player?

It feels really good - and to be back in England as well. It's a top club that has won a lot of trophies in the past - and will do so in the future we hope as well. I've got the trust of the manager and the club, which for me is very nice and I'm proud to be here.

How did you feel when you heard Liverpool were interested in you?

I felt really good because I wanted to come back to England one day. I knew sooner or later I would be back. Being back with Liverpool is even better because I can show the people what I can do. We've got the Europa League and lots of things to play for.

This will be the third time you've worked with Brendan Rodgers. How important was the boss in bringing you here?

He was very important. I wouldn't say it was the key, but most of it came from him. Even during last season, I spoke with him a lot. I'd text him and ask if he was okay and congratulated him on the results he got with Swansea. First of all it is a relationship of friendship, and afterwards it is a working one. That is more important than anything.

What is Brendan like to play for?

I used to play 4-3-3 with him and he is very good to play football for. It is great to play football for him because you can have fun and you can get results. I could see at Swansea the people loved him because the football was attractive. People like to see football (played) like this.

What can we expect to see from the Liverpool players next season under Brendan?

They will certainly see football players that want to win, and that will always work for the team rather than themselves. Liverpool wants to get results and that's what we'll try to do.

What sort of player would you describe yourself as?

I'd describe myself as a player that never gives up and I run a lot. I had difficult times at Chelsea when I was younger because I came from Italy. It was very difficult, I tried to be strong for myself and demonstrate to people I could do it. That is an achievement I have made and why I am here.

You've just come back from being with the Italy squad at the European Championships. Has that experience helped you develop as a player?

Of course. It was a big experience for me. I'm only 21 years old, so it was a good experience even if I didn't play. Getting to the final was even more experience because it's not something that happens every day. It will be great to bring it (the experience) with me.

I believe you have a special goal celebration Liverpool fans will want to see this season. Can you tell us a bit about it?

My celebration is a knife between the teeth. In Italy it means a warrior or someone who never gives up and will always get up if they fall down. At Swansea and Roma the fans liked it, so I hope to show it to Liverpool fans as well.

As a forward, how much are you looking forward to playing with Luis Suarez this season?

A lot because he is maybe another player who is similar to me because he works very hard in every game. I've watched a few games, and all of Europe wants him. Every player wants to play with him, so it will be a pleasure.

In coming to Liverpool, you're joining one of the biggest clubs in Europe. Are you aware of the club's history?

Yes, I am aware of it. I remember the Champions League final against AC Milan. It is very important to have this important past because you can bring it to the future and try to remake the past

New Signing

You've already played at Anfield once before in an FA Youth Cup tie in February 2009 - what do you remember about that night?

(Laughs) I remember we lost! We had a good team at Chelsea in the FA Youth Cup, but we lost. But the impression it left on me was very good because of the stadium's history. It's a dream for everyone to play at Anfield, so it was a very nice experience.

So are you excited about playing at Anfield every other week now this season?

Yes, every other week in a full stadium. It will be amazing. I know the fans are very warm and they're here for football.

What do you hope to achieve during your time at Liverpool?

I hope to achieve the maximum I can, by scoring goals, getting into the Champions League and all of the things the club also wants - and all the other players.

Finally, do you have a message for Liverpool fans?

There's not especially one, but I think with Brendan they will see good football!

Fabio Borini 49

YOU'LL NEVER WALK ALONE

LIVERPOOL
FOOTBALL CLUB

EST·1892

Lucas Leiva

Lucas Leiva has spoken of his desire to return to top form after recovering from a serious knee injury which ruled him out of the final six months of last season.

The Brazilian midfielder suffered anterior cruciate knee ligament damage at Chelsea in November and only made his comeback to competitive action as Liverpool kicked off their North America tour against Toronto in the summer.

Having worked tirelessly to overcome one of the most serious injuries in the game, Lucas is now looking forward to picking up where he left off before his nightmare began.

"I don't have too many experiences with injuries because fortunately I had none in my time at Liverpool previously, so it has been a learning process for me as well and I am very happy with the progress," said the Reds' No.21.

"I think I have progressed very well in terms of the knee, strength and fitness-wise.

"I am working every week and trying to improve every week and the main target is to be fit as soon as possible.

"I am confident I will be back at the same level because I know how hard I am working.

"The first four weeks I saw my knee it was very bad looking, and it comes through your head that you might not be at the same level you were before.

"But at the same time you see big players who had the same injury come back and be even better.

"There is no need for me to be scared. Rather than stay protecting myself, I need to work on my head as well, to come back and play the same way I was playing before.

"One of the things which made me strong in the team was how aggressive I was in tackles and things like that, so I cannot lose that."

Lucas admits he initially struggled to come to terms with his long-term lay-off – but he is now relishing the prospect of playing an integral role in Brendan Rodgers' new-look side.

"It has been very hard for me because I have never been out for a month so you can imagine five months when I can't play and only watch the game," he said.

"I just had to cope with the injury and the time. As soon as I got the injury I knew I would be out for many months and I started to think about other things.

"The most difficult period for me was when I was on crutches for two months, especially the first four weeks after the surgery when the knee was swollen.

"To be honest, for a few moments I thought I couldn't come back or even walk, because the way I looked at my knee I felt scared.

"But as soon as I started the rehab, it is unbelievable how your body reacts.

"My main target now is to be 100 per cent recovered and be okay to play a part in the season.

"I just have to be patient again; much of my life in Liverpool has been like that."

New boss Rodgers, meanwhile, has no doubts that his Brazilian midfielder has a big role to play this season and beyond.

"I have only been at the club a short period of time, and when I first arrived, everyone told me about how special he was as a player and a character, and he's even better when you meet him in real life and see how hard he works.

"The injury he's had is normally nine months before you get back at all, so he's back two months early. You only do that through one thing: sheer determination and hard work.

"I know that every day of his life he is fighting hard to get back, and as I said, he's not only a top footballer but a top guy as well.

"He is the ultimate professional. He is going to be a brilliant player for me in my career here at Liverpool and I'm looking forward to seeing him back fully fit."

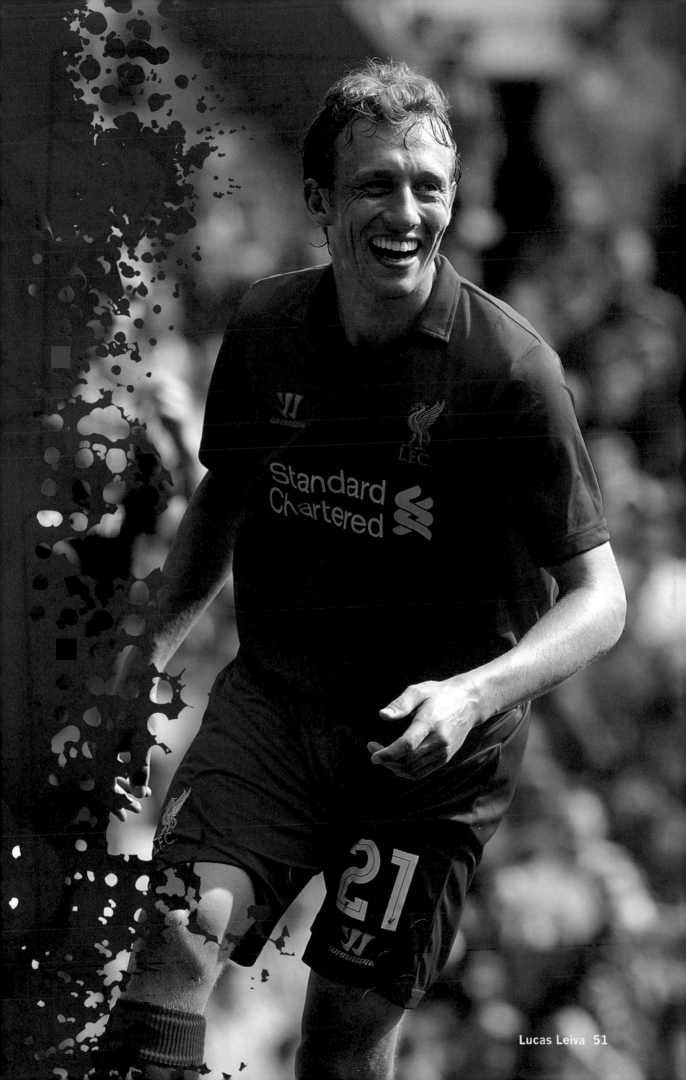

Lucas Leiva 51

LUIS SUAREZ
GOAL-DEN MOMENTS

A stunning Suarez strike helps the Reds to victory at the Britannia Stadium in the Carling Cup

Suarez is the match winner with this header to beat QPR

Luis nets with a header as the Reds go goal crazy against Brighton

Suarez levels the scores in the FA Cup semi final with a low finish past Howard

Jonjo Shelvey

Liverpool youngster Jonjo Shelvey celebrated the summer on the back of signing a new contract with the Reds.

After penning his new deal, the England youth international spoke to the club's official website about his delight – and about the future under new boss Brendan Rodgers.

Jonjo, congratulations. You must be delighted with your new deal...

I am really happy. Last season I was itching to try and push for a new contract. Now it's happened and I am ready to kick on again now.

How much of a boost is it for you to know that the club see you as part of the future?

It's lovely to know I am in the plans for the future. At the moment, it's just about getting things right each day and proving myself to the gaffer here. The gaffer and his way of playing will suit me down to the ground and hopefully I can be in his plans.

You've had a few weeks to reflect now - how do you look back on your form last season?

I think going away (on loan) to Blackpool helped me a lot. It gave me some experience, I scored some goals and I came back a better player. Kenny gave me a chance towards the latter stages of the season and I thought I showed what I can do.

In what ways do you think you've improved at Liverpool?

Tactically I have become a lot better and technically too. When you're working with people like Steven Gerrard and people like that, you're learning things day in, day out and it's an honour.

Are there any areas you'd like to improve upon?

There are still things in my game I want to work on and I'm going to keep doing that. On the physical side of my game, I'm going to be in the gym every day - and I've got to speak to the gaffer to see what else I can work on.

So you've got a new deal - what is your aim for the new season?

To start playing more games. I want to get into the first team and be in the starting XI on a permanent basis. That's going to be hard, but it's something I've got to work towards.

You touched upon it earlier, but you've had time working with Brendan Rodgers. What are your first impressions of him?

I think he's great. With all the passing drills he's doing, he's encouraging us to play all the time which is nice for a football player. Instead of doing a lot of long-distance running and things like that in pre-season, everything has been with a ball, which is more enjoyable. Everyone is enjoying training and looking forward to coming in.

Is that passing type of game something you feel will bring out the best in you?

I think so. I think it'll sharpen me up. The gaffer's also got a big thing about pressing the other teams hard, so I am trying to work on that side of my game as well.

What's the mood like amongst the rest of the lads with the new manager in charge?

Everyone is buzzing because he likes to play football. That's what people want to do and what fans want to see - nice, attractive football. Hopefully we can bring that to Anfield this year.

Overall, are you looking forward to this new season?

Yes, I'm very much looking forward to it. I'm buzzing to still be at Liverpool and I want to show the fans what I can do.

Jonjo Shelvey 55

Glen Johnson

Glen Johnson has welcomed the addition of youth to the Liverpool squad this season – and insists it's the responsibility of the experienced players to help them shine.

Raheem Sterling and Adam Morgan have tasted first team action so far after progressing through the ranks, and Johnson is confident it represents the sign of a promising future at Anfield.

"We've got a great bunch of lads and everyone makes everyone feel welcome," said the England international.

"Raheem is 17-years-old but you make him feel like one of the lads because he is and he deserves to be here. It makes him feel more comfortable - and more comfortable when he's going into games, which is going to help him and the team.

"You have to encourage the young lads. When I first came through, I had people like Stuart Pearce and other big players helping me.

"Raheem is a fantastic player as it is, so if he keeps working hard and doing the right things, he's going to be a great player."

Meanwhile, Johnson insists the Reds will enjoy success under new boss Brendan Rodgers – even if it doesn't arrive instantly.

"Anything new is going to take time to mould [together], but the lads are working hard every day to try and make the success come together," Johnson said.

"Everyone needs to be patient, including the players. We need to get on top of teams from the start and try and make it as difficult as possible for them for the 90 minutes.

"When Brendan is talking, you're so focused on what he's saying. He gets your attention 100 per cent. You can be in a meeting for half an hour with him, but it'll feel like 10 minutes.

"It's clear for everyone to see the way Brendan wants us to play. He did fantastic at Swansea and he's a fantastic coach."

Asked how he hopes to be reflecting on this campaign in May, Johnson added: "Another medal would be nice, but the objective would be to say we've finished in the top four. That would definitely be the main objective.

"It's possible. We've got a very good squad and the lads are pretty confident we can cause teams a lot of problems. If we take a few more chances than we did last season then we'll be there or thereabouts."

Glen Johnson 57

SPOT THE DIFFERENCES!

Can you spot the 8 differences in the picture below?

Answers on Page 61

GUESS WHO?

Can you guess who's in the pictures below?

1.

2.

3.

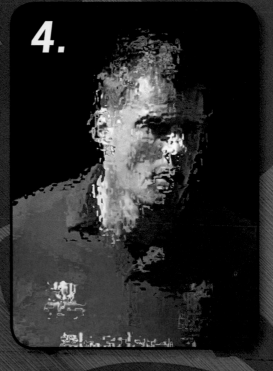

4.

Answers on Page 61

QUIZ ANSWERS

CROSSWORD Page 38

ACROSS

4 NEWCASTLE
5 SWANSEA
7 KUYT
8 URUGUAY
9 ROMA

DOWN

1 REINA
2 ISTANBUL
3 SEVEN
5 SCOTLAND
6 WARRIOR

WORDSEARCH Page 39

Y	L	K	N	A	H	S	I	R	G	P
N	J	G	K	P	N	S	J	O	E	D
H	N	F	T	R	T	I	R	I	R	K
S	N	M	O	A	T	Z	E	R	R	M
I	Y	T	N	W	E	D	H	R	A	J
L	K	B	Y	R	L	P	G	A	R	N
G	U	J	A	E	L	E	A	W	D	G
L	P	U	I	L	B	O	R	I	N	I
A	S	F	P	O	K	P	R	R	Y	D
D	N	X	K	D	B	M	A	R	K	R
A	M	C	T	L	T	Y	C	D	Z	F

SPOT THE DIFFERENCES
Page 58

GUESS WHO Page 59

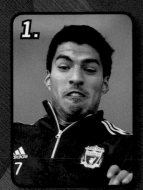

1.

Luis Suarez

2.

Brendan Rodgers

3.

Jay Spearing

4.

Jamie Carragher

How well did you do?

Where's our mascot, Mighty Red?

Can you spot him in the crowd below?